# TABLE OF CONTENTS

Page

CHAPTER

# CHAPTER 1

## INTRODUCTION

The year is 2010. Tribal leaders continue to dissent against the legitimate government of Sudan. They refuse to acknowledge their country's government. One of the more vicious tribal leaders is a man named Abdullah Omar. He starves his people by preventing delivery of food shipments from nongovernmental organizations. He has ordered the killings of innocent women and children in the past. His armed followers are motivated solely by money and fear of him. He has no ties to global terrorism. He is only a regional threat. He is preventing peace and stability in Sudan. It is believed Abdullah Omar is the tribe's center of gravity and without him the people will follow the country's legitimate government. The local government is incapable of dealing with this rogue tribal leader. The United States National Security Council debates courses of action to deal with Abdullah Omar and Sudan. Can the United States assassinate Abdullah Omar?

### Background

In this futuristic scenario, the threat comes from the army and terror controlled by a single individual. This threat is of important interest to the United States because of regional stability. The United States has been faced with threats from individuals throughout its history. Military leaders like Manuel Noriega, and Saddam Hussein and non-state actors like Osama bin Laden and Mohammed Farrah Aidid have threatened and continue to threaten the United States and its interests. The United States applies diplomatic, information, military, and economic instruments of power to deal with these threats. But these instruments of power affect more than just one individual. Can the

1

United States assassinate an individual who poses a threat to its national security and interests?

Currently, the answer is no. An executive order prohibits the United States government from conducting assassinations. In 1976, President Ford was the first to ban assassinations through his presidential directive, Executive Order 11905 (U.S. President 1976, 1).

The 1970s, leading up to the executive order outlawing assassination, was a time of moral self-righteousness in the aftermath of the Vietnam War. Americans were concerned over the alleged killings of innocent civilians, particularly women and children, in Vietnam. The American people did not understand their country's purpose and role in Vietnam. Then came the Watergate scandal. The ideas of constitutional rights and privacy came to the forefront.

The American public was fearful of becoming targets of the CIA's activities, especially electronic eavesdropping (Lowry 2002, 36). The CIA was involved in other scandals. The United States Senate, specifically the Church Committee, published a report on allegations of United States' involvement, either indirect or direct, in assassination plots against foreign political leaders (U.S. Congress, Senate 1975, 1). Congress and the American people were pushing for an end to the CIA's covert actions. Congress needed to legislate the CIA's activities. The answer was to establish a presidential directive requiring presidential approval for the CIA to conduct special activities. So Executive Order 11905 was enacted.

President Reagan reinforced the initial ban on assassinations by signing Executive Order 12333 on 4 December 1981 (U.S. President 1981, 1). President Reagan's directive stands today and states, "No persons employed by or acting on behalf of the United States Government shall engage in, or conspire to engage in, assassination" (U.S. President 1981, 18).

However, a presidential directive is considered a policy, not a law. Let us look at laws that address the topic of assassination. The Law of War states it is "permissible to kill an enemy in any place whatsoever" (Friedman 1972, 39). However, an assassin who acts treacherously violates both the law of nature and the law of nations (Friedman 1972, 40). The Law of War equates assassination to barbarism. The Hague Regulation, in Convention II, specifies further by saying it is "prohibited to kill or wound treacherously individuals belonging to the hostile nation or army" (Friedman 1972, 229).

The Department of the Army has adopted similar restrictions regarding assassination in their regulations dating back to 1863. United States Army General Order No. 100 states, "The law of war does not allow proclaiming either an individual belonging to the hostile army, or a citizen, or a subject of the hostile government an outlaw, who may be slain without trial by any captor, any more than the modern law of peace allows such international outlawry; on the contrary, it abhors such outrage . . . " (War Department 1863, 14). Field Manual 27-10 also addresses assassination in its law of land warfare. Current Army doctrine states, "It is especially forbidden to kill or wound treacherously individuals belonging to the hostile nation or army. This article is construed as prohibiting assassination, proscription, or outlawry of an enemy, or putting a price upon an enemy's head, as well as offering a reward for an enemy 'dead or alive'. It does not, however, preclude attacks on individual soldiers or officers of the enemy whether in

3

the zone of hostilities, occupied territory, or elsewhere" (Department of the Army 1956, 17).

Looking back even further into history, the prohibition of assassination was not a law, rather an informal contract between sovereigns. Leaders declared themselves exempt from attack as an agreement between gentlemen. This informal agreement precluded them from being targeted for assassination which would be deemed a violation of honor and justice (Zengel 1991, 126).

## Assumptions

There seems to be some debate over the exact definition of assassination. Most scholars agree that it is an illegal act committed for political purposes. This would negate the possibility that killing an average citizen on the street could qualify as assassination. The problem is that Executive Order 12333 and the United Nations Charter fail to define assassination. A good working definition is imperative.

*Webster's Collegiate Dictionary* defines assassination as "1. to murder by sudden or secret attack usu. for impersonal reasons. 2. to injure or destroy unexpectedly and treacherously" (*Webster's* 1984, 108). While researching this topic, the most commonly used definition of assassination is the "premeditated and intentional killing of a public figure accomplished violently and treacherously for a political purpose" (Pape 2002, 64).

This thesis uses the following definition of assassination: the premeditated and intentional killing of a protected person conducted treacherously for a political purpose. No definition specifies whether the country conducting an assassination needs to be in the midst of war, conflict, or peace. While it does specify killing for political purposes, it does not address the difference of conducting an assassination during peacetime versus wartime. Today the lines between war, conflict, and peace are often vague. Currently, Congress has not declared war even though the President has stated the United States is engaged in a war on terrorism. Congress has not declared war since World War II but most would agree that Vietnam and Korea were, in fact, wars. This thesis argues that assassination is not time specific, meaning it is not dependent on war or peace.

## Key Definitions

Assassination. The premeditated and intentional killing of a protected person conducted treacherously for a political purpose.

Asymmetric Warfare. Acting, organizing, and thinking differently from opponents to maximize relative strengths, exploit opponents' weaknesses or gain greater freedom of action (Metz 2001, 3).

Center of Gravity. Those characteristics, capabilities, or sources of power from which a military force derives its freedom of action, physical strength, or will to fight ( Joint Chiefs of Staff 2001).

Protected Person. A Head of State, Head of Government, or Minister of Foreign Affairs (Ku 1979, 854).

## Research Methodology

The research design will incorporate several techniques including a literature review on assassination; review of current United States policy and international law; analysis of the advantages and disadvantages of assassination; a case study using the country of Israel; potential threats to the United States; and recommendations to deal with those threats. The primary question is: Can the United States assassinate an individual

5

who poses a threat to its national security and interests? To answer the primary question, the following secondary questions must be addressed:

1. What is the current United States policy regarding assassinations?

2. Why was this policy enacted?

3. Has the United States engaged in assassinations as a tool of foreign policy?

4. What is international law regarding assassinations?

5. What are other countries' policies regarding assassination?

6. What is the effect when other countries conduct assassinations?

7. What are the potential threats to the United States and its interests?

8. Would assassination truly eliminate any threats to the United States?

## Significance of the Study

Are Executive Order 12333 and its ban on assassination applicable today? Twenty-five years ago it may have been necessary, but it may need revision to support today's war on terrorism. Terrorism is no longer something that happens to foreigners thousands of miles from their borders. On 11 September 2001, terrorists attacked this country on its soil, causing more casualties than the Japanese attack on Pearl Harbor. America has long defeated conventional threats. Today this country is faced with asymmetric threats from rogue nations and non-state actors. In his State of the Union address in 2002, President Bush identified North Korea, Iran, and Iraq as the Axis of Evil. The National Security Council has many tools, instruments of power, at its disposal to use in dealing with foreign nations and flexing its international muscle. Maybe assassination is just another tool to deal with threats to this country's security and interests. Can the United States assassinate an individual who poses a threat to its national security and interests?

## Conclusion

This chapter has introduced the topic of assassination. The hypothetical scenario of Abdullah Omar explores the possibility of targeting one individual to eliminate a threat to United States interests. The next chapter will present a review of the literature regarding assassination.

CHAPTER 2

LITERATURE REVIEW

<u>Introduction</u>

This chapter reviews the literature regarding assassinations. First, it will address

current United States policy and international law. Then it lists the literature discussing

the pros and cons regarding assassination. Finally, it will address the use of assassination

by other countries, specifically Israel, and its impacts both politically and militarily.

<u>Background</u>

The Department of the Army has adopted regulations prohibiting assassination

dating back to 1863. United States Army General Order No. 100, also known as the

Lieber Code, states, "The law of war does not allow proclaiming either an individual

belonging to the hostile army, or a citizen, or a subject of the hostile government an

outlaw, who may be slain without trial by any captor, any more than the modern law of

peace allows such international outlawry; on the contrary, it abhors such outrage. The

sternest retaliation should follow the murder committed in consequence of such

proclamation, made by whatever authority. Civilized nations look with horror upon offers

of rewards for the assassination of enemies as relapses into barbarism" (War Department

1863, 14).

The Army's current doctrine also addresses the prohibition on assassination. The

law of land warfare addresses assassination in Field Manual 27-10, its current version

dates back to 1956. This doctrine states, "It is especially forbidden to kill or wound

treacherously individuals belonging to the hostile nation or army. This article is construed

as prohibiting assassination, proscription, or outlawry of an enemy, or putting a price upon an enemy's head, as well as offering a reward for an enemy 'dead or alive'. It does not, however, preclude attacks on individual soldiers or officers of the enemy whether in the zone of hostilities, occupied territory, or elsewhere" (Department of the Army 1956, 17). The United States Army has clearly banned assassination dating back to 1863.

What does international law say regarding assassination? Article XXIII of the Law of War states, ". . . it is especially prohibited to kill or wound treacherously individuals belonging to the hostile nation or army" (Friedman 1972, 229). Article CXLVIII further states, "The Law of War does not allow proclaiming either an individual belonging to the hostile army, or a citizen, or a subject of the hostile government, an outlaw, who may be slain without trial by any captor, any more than the modern law of peace allows such intentional outlawry; on the contrary, it abhors such outrage. The sternest retaliation should follow the murder committed in consequence of such proclamation, made by whatever authority. Civilized nations look with horror upon offers of rewards for the assassination of enemies as relapses into barbarism" (Friedman 1972, 184). Assassination is clearly a violation of the law of war and the law of nations.

In 1945, the Charter of the United Nations was signed prohibiting assassination (United Nations 1945, 1). Article 2(4) states: "All Members shall refrain in their international relations from the threat or use of force against the territorial integrity or political independence of any state, or in any other manner inconsistent with the Purposes of the United Nations" (United Nations 1945, 1).

Article 51 of the United Nations Charter addresses a nation's right to self-defense. It states "Nothing in the present Charter shall impair the inherent right of individual or collective self-defense if an armed attack occurs against a Member of the United Nations,

9

until the Security Council has taken measures necessary to maintain international peace and security. Measures taken by Members in the exercise of this right of self-defense shall be immediately reported to the Security Council and shall not in any way affect the authority and responsibility of the Security Council under the present Charter to take at any time such action as it deems necessary in order to maintain or restore international peace and security" (United Nations 1945, 3).

On 14 December 1973, The United Nations also adopted the Convention on the Prevention and Punishment of Crimes Against Internationally Protected Persons, Including Diplomatic Agents (Ku 1979, 853). Article 1 of this convention defines internationally protected persons as Heads of State, Heads of Government, or Ministers of Foreign Affairs (Ku 1979, 854). Article 2 directs treaty nations to make assassination of internationally protected persons punishable under their own domestic law (Ku, 1979, 855).

In 1976, President Ford signed Executive Order 11905, the predecessor to Executive Order 12333 (U.S. President 1976, 1). It stated, "No employee of the United States Government shall engage in, or conspire to engage in, political assassination" (U.S. President 1976, 14). Assassination is only referenced in this singular sentence.

This original executive order was enacted in response to pressure from Congress, specifically a Senate Committee. "Alleged Assassination Plots Involving Foreign Leaders" is a Senate report of a committee studying governmental operations with respect to intelligence activities. The committee was directed to investigate intelligence activities to determine if they were illegal, improper, or unethical. The committee investigated alleged United States involvement in the following assassination plots: Patrice Lumumba of the Congo; Fidel Castro of Cuba; Rafael Trujillo of the Dominican Republic; Ngo Dinh Diem of South Vietnam; and General Rene Schneider of Chile (U.S. Congress, Senate 1975, 4). Their findings were as follows: "(1) Officials of the United States Government initiated plots to assassinate Patrice Lumumba and Fidel Castro; (2) No foreign leaders were killed as a result of assassination plots initiated by officials of the United States; (3) American officials encouraged and were privy to coup plots which resulted in the deaths of Trujillo, Diem, and Schneider; (4) The plots occurred in a Cold War atmosphere perceived to be of crisis proportions; (5) American officials have exaggerated notions about their ability to control the actions of coup leaders; and (6) CIA officials made use of known underworld figures in assassination efforts" (U.S. Congress, Senate 1975, 255).

The Senate Committee determined that assassination was a violation of American ideals. "The United States must not adopt the tactics of the enemy. Means are as important as ends. Crisis makes it tempting to ignore the wise restraints that make men free. But each time we do so, each time the means we use are wrong, our inner strength, the strength which makes us free, is lessened" (U.S. Congress, Senate 1975, 285). The committee concluded that the United States should not engage in assassination and called for formal legislation prohibiting assassination.

What is the current United States policy regarding assassination? President Reagan signed Executive Order 12333 on 4 December 1981 (U.S. President 1981, 1). This order delineated the duties and responsibilities of the various United States intelligence agencies. This directive was designed to protect the United States, its national interests and citizens, from foreign security threats. It also prohibited

11

assassinations by stating, "No person employed by or acting on behalf of the United States Government shall engage in, or conspire to engage in, assassination" (U.S. President 1981, 18). This one sentence is the only reference to assassination in the executive order.

## For Assassination

There are two opposing camps with regards to assassination. Those in favor view assassination as lawful, proportionate, and less of an impact to the people of the targeted country. They argue, why should the citizens of a country suffer for the acts of one when targeting one would save bloodshed. The following articles represent those in favor of the United States conducting assassinations.

Major Tyler Harder, a United States Army Judge Advocate General Corps Officer, researched the executive order on assassination. In "Time to Repeal the Assassination Ban of Executive Order 12,333 (sic): A Small Step in Clarifying Current Law," he calls for a repeal of the executive order saying the order leads to confusion. The confusion begins with the definition of assassination and the absence of a definition in the executive order. The author believes there should be a wartime and peacetime definition of assassination. Harder defines assassination during wartime as "the targeting of an individual by treacherous means" and during peacetime as "a political murder of a specifically targeted figure" (Harder 2002, 6).

Harder's main argument to repeal the ban on assassination is that it creates artificial limits on the United States' ability to respond to threats and cites several examples. The first example centers on the concern over targeting Qadhafi's home and headquarters in 1986. Intelligence had reported Libyan involvement in the terrorist

12

bombing of a nightclub in Germany and future planned attacks on United States'

facilities worldwide (Harder 2002, 21). Although there was some debate over whether

this could be considered assassination, targeting Qadhafi was finally judged lawful. Not

only was he considered a combatant by virtue of his position, Article 51 gives the United

States the right to self-defense against future and continuing threats.

Harder's second example is the debate over targeting Saddam Hussein during the

Gulf War in 1991. As the leader of the Iraqi military and thus a combatant, Hussein was a

legitimate and lawful target regardless of where he is physically located on the battlefield.

He caveats it by saying as long as it was not accomplished treacherously.

Harder's last example is the failure to target Manuel Noriega in 1989. The United

States originally failed to support a coup by a Panamanian military officer based on the

Senate's concern of the CIA's support for foreigners conducting assassinations (Harder

2002, 31). The Department of Justice later ruled that Executive Order 12333 "did not

prevent US assistance to coup plotters in foreign countries, provided the coup's primary

objective was not the death of a political leader" (Harder 2002, 31). The coup failed and

Noriega remained in power. This does not imply that support of another military regime

would have encouraged democracy. Months later Operation Just Cause ousted Noriega

from power but with cost of American soldiers' lives.

Harder believes there is no need for Executive Order 12333 because assassination

is prohibited by federal statutes and international law. He says Executive Order 12333 is

redundant and unnecessary and repealing the ban would not make assassination legal, just

eliminate the confusion and give the United States the flexibility in dealing with current

and potential threats (Harder 2002, 38).

The United States Army War College Quarterly featured an article by Matthew Pape, a Texas attorney, titled "Can We Put the Leaders of the 'Axis of Evil' in the Crosshairs?" Published after the 11th of September attacks, this article focuses on dealing with the rogue states identified as the axis of evil by President Bush in his State of the Union address in January 2002. He specifically addresses removing Saddam Hussein as a solution to the Iraqi threat. He also argues eliminating leaders like Manuel Noriega and Saddam Hussein would have prevented the use of massive military force in 1989 and 1990, respectively.

The author identifies four ways the President could usurp the executive order and legally assassinate a hostile foreign leader. First, the President can ask Congress to declare war on the hostile nation and target its leader to remove military command and control. Second, the President can target a foreign leader in self-defense in accordance with Article 51 of the United Nations Charter. Third, the President can refer to the assassination as "restoring the legitimate government or apprehending an international terrorist" (Pape 2002, 67). Pape considers this option to be the most lawful. Fourth, the President can revise the executive order to allow open or secretive assassinations. However, usurping the system could have both international and domestic effects. Internationally, lifting the ban on assassination could lead to international instability because foreign nations would be unsure of how the United States would act.

Domestically, opponents of assassination feel it violates the principles on which this nation was founded. He argues the ethical difference between assassinating for ideology versus those who threaten American lives. He concludes that assassination is an "option in the arsenal of presidential constitutional authority" and is proportionate when

14

the nation is threatened by one person which is applicable in today's war on terrorism (Pape 2002, 70).

Richard Lowry finds legal and moral justification in killing enemies like Saddam Hussein and Osama bin Laden in his article, "A View to a Kill." Legally, he argues that for an assassination to be unlawful it has to be conducted treacherously. Any method considered lawful for attacking an enemy is also considered lawful for attacking its leader. Treachery implies the use of perfidious means. He offers the example of bin Laden's use of assassins posing as journalists to kill Northern Alliance leader Ahmed Massoud as a case of perfidy (Lowry 2002, 38). Morally, he views assassination as superior to other means of trying to oust dictators. Options like economic sanctions just punish the innocent civilians of the targeted country. Lowry's solution is to define assassination in the executive order, "making it clear that it does not forbid targeting a regime's military elite" (Lowry 2002, 38).

While attending the Naval War College, Lieutenant Colonel Keller authored "Targeting the Head of State During the Gulf Conflict, A Legal Analysis". As the title reads, this paper is solely a legal argument not a moral one. He reviews Executive Order 12333, the Hague and Geneva Conventions, and the United Nations Charter. His legal argument centers on the right to self-defense and preemptive self-defense. He asks whether the United States Armed Forces could kill a foreign leader during armed conflict, if they had previously identified the leader as a target. He determines that the right of self-defense authorizes the attack against any state leader as long as his illegal conduct presents a continuing risk to the vital interests of the United States. During armed conflict, the United States may target a foreign leader who proves invaluable to the

15

enemy's armed forces. Keller concludes that "with the National Command Authorities' approval, General Schwarzkopf could have designated Saddam Hussein as a specific target during the Gulf Conflict without violating Executive Order 12333, the Hague Convention, the Geneva Convention, or the United Nations Charter" (Keller 1992, 25).

Lieutenant Colonel Irvin researched the topic of assassination while attending the United States Army War College and published an article titled "Political Assassination, the Strategic Precision Weapon of Choice." He argues that assassination could be the ultimate precision weapon to counter the rogue states and non-state entities that would wage an asymmetric war. Irvin explores the global, historical, moral, and legal reasons assassination is the strategic precision weapon of choice. Globally, other nations such as Israel, United Kingdom, and Egypt conduct assassinations (Irvin 2002, 2). The United States does not condemn its allies' use of assassination. Morally, assassination minimizes collateral damage thus limiting greater death and destruction. Legally, assassination equates to preemptive self-defense, which is governed under Article 51 of the United Nations Charter. Irvin recommends the executive order be written to reflect as follows: "The Central Intelligence Agency in cooperation with the Department of Defense may evaluate, plan, and propose for approval to the President of the United States as a means of pre-emptive self-defense the assassination of persons know to be of threat to the national security, the safety, the welfare, and the way of life of the American people" (Irvin 2002, 16). He feels the post-9/11 American public is ready to see the President lift the ban on assassination (Irvin 2002, 1).

The Honorable Caspar Weinberger served as Secretary of Defense under President Reagan from 1981 to 1987. In his article, "When Can We Target the Leaders?',

16

Weinberger asks whether the United States can eliminate or jail brutal aggressors. The question involves both moral and legal issues. He sees moral justification in assassinating leaders because it often ends wars and saves soldiers' lives. It is also legally justified if the leader is the commander of the armed forces, thus making him a combatant. To clarify the executive order, he recommends adding, "the otherwise legal targeting of lawful combatants in armed conflict, including all members of any enemy nation's or organization's operational chain of command is not assassination and is not forbidden by this order" (Weinberger 2001, 24). So the answer to his question of whether or not the United States should eliminate or jail brutal aggressors is yes (Weinberger 2001, 21).

In "War By Assassination," John Filiss argues that warfare should not consist of clashes between soldiers but rather against the perpetrators themselves. He offers the following hypothetical scenarios. If Nation A declares war on Nation B, then Nation B should target the leadership of Nation A. Although he does see the possibility of Nation A retaliating against the leadership of Nation B. He proposes some ideas of what a system of war by assassination would look like. It would involve something like a bounty system, either large sums of money or reward of goods. Special forces, either governmental or private, would implement assassination policies and be guaranteed safe haven. This method of war by assassination would target the individuals responsible for creating the war in the first place. While being direct and less tragic than a conventional war, this would deter the perpetrators (for example the country's leadership) and provide an incentive to avoid war. A country's leadership would be more apt to use diplomacy to avoid the more personal system of war by assassination (Filiss 2002, 1).

Louis Rene Beres, a professor of International Law at Purdue University, has written several articles on the topic of assassination. In "Assassination: Getting Them First," he discusses the new National Security Strategy released by President Bush in late 2002. It calls for the right of preemption, a right known as anticipatory self-defense under international law. Assassination is normally a violation of international law during both peacetime and wartime. He describes conditions that must be met for assassination to be classified as preemptive. First, assassination must target only those leaders responsible. Second, it needs to meet the rules of discrimination, proportionality, and military necessity. Third, intelligence reports must confirm enemy preparations for an attack. Fourth, assassination must prevent the attack with less harm to civilians.

Beres believes President Bush's strategy of preemption should include limited rights of assassination. He argues that assassination would be lawful if it prevented nuclear or biological attack on large civilian populations. He concludes, "whenever assassination is judged the most efficient and least harmful form of preemption, it should be accepted with regret but also with determination" (Beres 2003, 2). He closes with a list of over twenty-five assassinations of twentieth century leaders from the President of the United States to the King of Iraq (Beres 2003, 1).

<u>Against Assassination</u>

Generally, those opposed to assassination view it as a violation of American values, democratic ideals, and the golden rule. The golden rule, "do unto others as you would have them do unto you," raises the question of possible retribution. If the United States targets foreign leaders for political purposes, then other countries could in turn target the President of the United States. The following literary documents are opposed to the United States conducting assassinations.

Lieutenant Colonel Bolchoz researched the topic of assassination while attending the United States Army War College and authored "Center of Gravity: Justification for Assassination?" His paper asks whether identifying a leader as a center of gravity gives a nation the right to target that leader for assassination. His argument against assassination centers on the moral aspect. He views the United States not just as the only world power, but as a moral leader. He cites the Senate Committee's report saying "traditional values of fair play should guide all American activities on the international scene" (Bolchoz 1999, 14). He also feels assassination could threaten our democratic way of life because of possible retribution against our leaders. The required increase in security around our leaders could cause a decrease in access between elected officials and the American public.

Besides being politically and morally wrong, Bolchoz sees political assassination as too difficult and too risky. Too difficult because of the amount of resources required to track and locate the target. And too risky because you are not assured the assassination will accomplish the desired end state. He views assassination as a short-term solution that does not assure the protection of American interests. His research concludes that "while legally acceptable, political assassination is far too risky and costly, is morally unacceptable, and should not be an appropriate action for the United States, either as an option or as a deterrent" (Bolchoz 1999, 2). The latter far outweigh the legal justification. Bolchoz calls for formal legislation banning assassination to clarify United States policy (Bolchoz 1999, 20).

The Naval Postgraduate School in Monterrey, California published a document titled "Bullets With Names: The Deadly Dilemma." This thesis, written by Roger Herbert, Jr., examines the policy dilemma caused by national security threats like terrorists. His paper centers on six practical and philosophical arguments. First, assassination is a highly complex operation because of the security surrounding military and political leadership. Second, who would conduct the assassination? Third, history suggests that assassination does not accomplish its purpose. Fourth, the identity and character of the successor is unknown. Fifth, assassination invites retaliation in kind. Sixth, assassination contradicts democratic norms and may weaken American credibility. Based on these arguments, Herbert draws two major conclusions. "First, assassination cannot support long-term US policy goals or warfighting efforts. Second, while assassination has no place in the US warfighting arsenal, the assassination ban itself has become dysfunctional and requires reevaluation" (Herbert 1992, ix).

Boyd M. Johnson, III examines the ways a President can circumvent the executive order and its ban on assassination. In "Executive Order 12,333 (sic): The Permissibility of an American Assassination of a Foreign Leader," he describes the four ways to usurp the order because the ban on assassination is solely written in the executive order. His article focuses solely on the legal not moral issues of assassination. The President may: (1) declare open war; (2) broadly construe Article 51 of the United Nations Charter and interpret criminal acts as legitimizing self-defense; (3) narrowly construe Executive Order 12333; and (4) repeal or amend the order, or permit Congress to do the same (Johnson 1992, 417). He applies these four loopholes to the Persian Gulf War and determines that President Bush would have been legally justified in targeting Saddam

20

Hussein. Johnson calls for Congressional legislation to remove the loopholes in the executive order (Johnson 1992, 434).

The article, "Evil in the Crosshairs," debates the National Security Council's next targets in the war on terrorism (Thomas and Barry 2001, 12). During the National Security Council's meetings, officials never discuss the word assassination; they refer to "taking out 'command and control' elements, structures and nodes, and of striking 'strategically decisive' blows" (Thomas and Barry 2001, 12). Administration lawyers ruled that assassination to preempt future attacks is lawful only in wartime, not peacetime (Thomas and Barry 2001, 12).

These authors argue against assassination plots for several reasons. First, conducting assassinations outside United States borders affect host nation sovereignty. Host countries prefer their own police and intelligence forces to capture or eliminate terrorists rather than American hit squads. The second argument is that assassination plots typically fail. They cite the examples of the CIA's failed attempts to assassinate Fidel Castro in the 1960s. Lastly, past history of moral compromises in Vietnam, specifically citing the Phoenix Program, included the assassinations of thousands of Viet Cong and their sympathizers.

The authors do not want the United States to conduct assassinations, thus legitimizing it as a tool of foreign policy. The international community could then be justified in targeting American leaders. This article also addresses Israel's assassination policy and its failure to stop terrorism. They cite the example of Israel hunting down and killing the murderers of Israeli athletes during the 1972 Olympic Games. They argue that Israel's open policy has led to a vicious cycle of tit-for-tat (Thomas and Barry 2001, 20).

21

Patrick Buchanan's article, "Do We Have a License to Kill?", debates President Bush's authority to direct the CIA to kill foreign leaders and conduct regime changes. He specifically addresses Saddam Hussein and Iraq, but asks whether the United States also has the right to conduct regime changes in other axis of evil nations such as Iran and North Korea. By allowing such United States action, he argues other countries could do the same. He cites examples like John F. Kennedy's contract on Fidel Castro which resulted in Kennedy's assassination, not Castro's. Also former President Bush's targeting of Saddam Hussein during Desert Storm resulted in an assassination attempt on President Bush in 1993. Buchanan concludes that the president needs to "convince his countrymen that Iraq's regime must be overthrown, and that Congress authorize the president to go to war to overthrow it" (Buchanan 2002, 2). This action would be both legitimate and constitutional as opposed to targeting the leader for assassination (Buchanan 2002, 1).

Doug Cassel is the Northwestern University's director of the Center for International Human Rights. In his article, "Repercussions: An Eye for an Eye," he refers to assassination as an "equal-opportunity weapon" because it is a tool to be used by any country (Cassel 2003, 1). He mentions a Presidential secret post-9/11 directive allowing the CIA to target suspected terrorists and cites the example of the CIA's drone aircraft firing a missile and killing a suspected Al Qaeda leader in Yemen (Cassel 2003, 3). The United States Department of Defense referred to this action as a successful tactical operation as compared to using the word assassination when other countries like Israel do it (Cassel 2003, 3). The world, including the United States, condemns Israel for targeting Palestinian terrorists. The executive order bans assassinations of foreign political leaders, not military commanders or suspected terrorists. Although there is pressure to revise the order, Cassel thinks the administration should not allow itself to fall back into the "repugnant practice of targeting foreign leaders," especially when they can be arrested (Cassel 2003, 1).

## Israel's Use of Assassination

To fully research the use of assassination as an instrument of foreign policy, its use by countries other than the United States must be addressed. Countries like the United Kingdom, Israel, and Egypt conduct assassinations. For purpose of this thesis, only assassination conducted by Israel will be discussed.

Beres' article, "Assassination of Terrorists May Be Law-Enforcing," addresses the assassination of Fathi Shiqaqi, leader of the terrorist group Islamic Holy War, in 1995. He argues that Israel was justified to assassinate the leader of a group dedicated to mass killings of Israelis. Israel had jurisdiction in this matter because Shiqaqi's crimes were directed at them and the punishment fit the crime. International law prefers to deal with terrorists through extradition and prosecution. However, the world lacks an international criminal court to deal with terrorists. Some nations even refuse to extradite terrorists, but instead harbor them. Beres concludes that assassination of terrorists, known as common enemies of humankind, can be judged as law-enforcing (Beres 1995, 1).

Tarik Kafala addresses Israel's open assassination policy in his article titled "Israel's Assassination Policy." The current Israeli Government continues the tradition of assassinating individuals it believes pose a threat to Israel and its citizens. He cites examples in Israel's history like the assassination of the Palestinian Liberation Organization's military leader and second-in-command in 1987 (Kafala 2001, 2). This policy is being criticized both domestically and internationally, mostly by human rights organizations. Such opposition feels the use of assassination "undermines the rule of law and fuels the cycle of violence in the region" (Kafala 2001, 3).

Jack Kelley wrote an article published in USA Today titled "'We're Going to Get Them': Israel Hunts Terrorists Amid Controversy." This article addresses the violence in the Israeli-Palestinian conflict and the controversy surrounding the Israeli targeted killings and the Palestinian suicide bombers. While Israel is committed to protecting its people and refers to these killings as preemptive strikes, Palestine is committed to using violence to force Israel out of the West Bank. While seventy-five percent of Israelis support their tactics, sixty-eight percent of Americans disapproved of the targeted killings (Kelley 2001, 2). Human rights groups are obviously opposed saying Israel's targeted killings violate the Hague Convention. Kelley says Israel uses Palestinian informants to track suspected militants. Then the killings are conducted by agents of Israel's elite Duvdevan (Kelley 2001, 3). These undercover assassins dress as Arab men and women, speak in local dialects, and have a working knowledge of the Koran (Kelley 2001, 3).

In "Jewish Assassination and Media Doublethink," Michael Hoffman blames the media for supporting Israelis in the Israeli-Palestinian conflict. He asks why, when Jews kill, it is called everything but assassination in the media. Terms that are used include targeted killings, military raids, retaliation, liquidation, interception, picking out targets for killings, actions to prevent the killing of Jews, and singling out Palestinians for death (Hoffman 2001, 2). The author sees not only media support but also support from high-ranking United States officials like Bush, Cheney, and Powell. Hoffman concludes, "the media concoct, on their editorial and news pages, a tenor of acceptance and advocacy for

24

state-sponsored Israeli assassinations, for the ethnic cleansing of the Palestinians"
(Hoffman 2001, 4).

## Conclusion

This chapter presented a review of the literature regarding assassination. First, it listed the literature reflecting current United States policy and international law prohibiting assassination. Second, the literature addressing the advantages and disadvantages of assassination were detailed. Then articles reflecting Israel's use of assassination were presented. The next chapter will present the research methodology used to research this topic.

# CHAPTER 3

## RESEARCH METHODOLOGY

### Introduction

This chapter addresses the research design to be followed in researching this thesis topic. The research methodology utilized incorporates several techniques including a literature review on assassinations; review of current United States policy and international law; analysis of the advantages and disadvantages of assassination; a case study on Israel's use of assassination; potential threats to the United States, and recommendations to deal with those threats.

### Methodology

The research methodology for this thesis is a four-step process. This methodology is designed to answer those questions presented in chapter 1. The primary question is "Can the United States assassinate an individual who poses a threat to its national security and interests?" To reiterate the secondary questions:

1. What is the current United States policy regarding assassinations?

2. Why was this policy enacted?

3. Has the United States engaged in assassinations as a tool of foreign policy?

4. What is international law regarding assassinations?

5. What are other countries' policies regarding assassination?

6. What is the effect when other countries conduct assassinations?

7. What are the potential threats to the United States and its interests?

8. Would assassination truly eliminate any threats to the United States?

## Step 1 Literature Review

The literature review consisted of five parts: current United States policy and international law; the historical perspective surrounding its implementation; pros of assassination; cons of assassination; and other country's use of assassination. The results of this literature review were presented in detail in chapter 2.

The review of current United States policy and international law governing assassination was critical to researching this topic. Current United States policy banning assassination prevents its use by the United States government regardless of its use as an instrument of foreign policy. International law prohibiting assassination makes its use by the United States government a violation both domestically and internationally.

The historical perspective was necessary to understand the reasons surrounding the implementation of United States policy. In 1976, the United States was faced with the conventional threats of a Cold War as opposed to the asymmetric threats from rogue nations and leaders today. The question is whether it is still applicable today, twenty-five years after its implementation.

The pros and advantages of assassination are an important part of studying whether or not the United States should engage in such conduct. The arguments in favor of assassination view it as lawful, proportionate, and less of an impact to the people of the targeted country.

The cons and disadvantages of assassination also assist in determining whether or not the United States should assassinate threats to its citizens or interests. The arguments opposed to assassination include it being a violation of American values, democratic ideals, and the golden rule.

Other country's use of assassination provides insights into how other countries deal with threats to their national security and interests. Countries like the United Kingdom, Israel, and Egypt have long-standing and open assassination policies.

## Step 2 Analysis

This step involved examination of current United States policy and international law, an analysis of the pros and cons of assassination, and its use by Israel. This step would provide valuable information in dealing with the threats outlined in step three. This analysis will address the following secondary questions:

1. What is the current United States policy regarding assassinations?

2. Why was this policy enacted?

3. Has the United States engaged in assassinations as a tool of foreign policy?

4. What is international law regarding assassinations?

5. What are other countries' policies regarding assassination?

6. What is the effect when other countries conduct assassinations?

## Step 3 Threats

In this step, the potential threats to the United States and its interests were determined. Threats range from conventional to asymmetric. The scope of threats could be one individual, one nation, multiple nations, religion, or ideology. This step addresses the question: What are the potential threats to the United States and its interests?

## Step 4 Synthesis

Based on the threats outlined in step three, the question of assassination would be applied to each. The question is: Would assassination eliminate the threat of X to the United States? Each threat would be addressed on a case-by-case basis to determine its outcome. In this last step, recommendations would be made based on whether or not assassination would eliminate it as a threat.

## Conclusion

This chapter has addressed the research design to be utilized when researching this thesis topic. The research methodology has incorporated several techniques including a literature review, analysis of the advantages and disadvantages of assassination, and conclusions based on that analysis. The next chapter will discuss the analysis of the research.

# CHAPTER 4

## ANALYSIS

### Introduction

This chapter presents the analysis of this thesis topic. The legal and moral arguments of assassination will be discussed. First, the definition of assassination must be scrutinized. Second, current United States policy and international law will be analyzed to fully understand the legal implications of assassination. Then the advantages and disadvantages of assassination will be discussed in detail. Israel and its open assassination policy will serve as a case study. Next, the potential threats to the United States and its interests will be determined. Lastly, the question of assassination will be applied to each potential threat to ascertain whether or not it would eliminate it as a threat.

### Defining Assassination

Neither Executive Order 12333 nor international law defines assassination. This leads to much debate. Most would agree assassination is the killing of a public figure for political purposes. This would mean the killing of an average citizen qualifies as murder, not assassination.

Webster's Collegiate Dictionary defines assassination, "1. to murder by sudden or secret attack usu. for impersonal reasons. 2. to injure or destroy unexpectedly and treacherously" (Webster's 1984, 108). Matthew Pape, a Texas attorney who has written extensively on assassination, defined assassination as "the premeditated and intentional killing of a public figure accomplished violently and treacherously for a political purpose" (Pape 2002, 64). For purpose of this thesis, the use of the word assassination means the premeditated and intentional killing of a protected person conducted treacherously for a political purpose.

Let us examine this definition. Premeditation requires prior planning. Assassination is therefore not killing on the spur of the moment, in a fit of rage. Intentional also implies that the killing was done deliberately and not accidentally. The definition uses the term "protected person" rather than "public figure." The term public figure could be misconstrued to mean any famous person, politician, or even an entertainer. So instead of using the term public figure, assassination only applies to protected persons. According to a United Nations Convention, protected persons are defined as Heads of State, Heads of Government, or Ministers of Foreign Affairs (Ku 1979, 854).

Treachery implies a breach of confidence according to Schmitt, a professor and scholar of the law of assassination (Harder 2002, 4). For example, a combatant sneaking into an enemy camp and killing one of its military leaders would not be considered treacherous. However, if the same combatant was wearing the enemy's uniform, thus breaching confidence, this would be considered treacherous. Another example of perfidy would be fabricating a surrender to gain an advantage over the enemy (Keller 1992, 8). And lastly, the killing must be conducted for a political purpose, not for personal reasons, in order to qualify as assassination. The person conducting the assassination may be part of an organized group or may be acting alone, but the focus of the killing would be to eliminate a person with differing political views.

Let us put the definition to the test with a couple of our current adversaries. An intentional and treacherous killing of Kim Jong Il would qualify as assassination. He is the Head of State of North Korea and, therefore, a protected person under the mandates of the United Nations. Osama bin Laden, however, would not qualify as a protected person under the United Nations definition. He is head of a terrorist organization, not a head of state.

The definition of assassination has not only caused confusion, it has also prevented the United States military from legitimately targeting its enemies. An excellent example would be the failure to eliminate Saddam Hussein during Desert Storm. Killing Saddam Hussein would not have met all the conditions mentioned earlier and therefore would not have been an assassination. Targeting him would qualify as premeditated and intentional. It also would have been conducted for a political purpose, for example withdrawal of Iraqi forces from Kuwait. But he is not only Head of State, he is also the leader of the Iraqi Military which makes him a lawful combatant. Photographs and camera footage during the war even showed him carrying a sidearm. Regardless of where he was physically located on the battlefield, he could have been legitimately targeted to undermine the enemy's command and control. There were many options in targeting him. First, the United States could have bombed a site where he was located. Or the United States could have sent in a Special Forces team to kill him. As long as the killing was not done treacherously, it would not have been an assassination. These would have been legitimate courses of action as long as there was not a breach of confidence.

Confusion over the definition of assassination has prevented the United States from legitimately eliminating its threats. The problem starts with the failure of Executive Order 12333 and international law to define assassination.

## The Legal Argument

Current United States policy regarding assassination is specified under Executive Order 12333, dated 4 December 1981. It states, "No persons employed by or acting on behalf of the United States Government shall engage in, or conspire to engage in, assassination" (U.S. President 1981, 18). This executive order clearly bans the government from assassinating persons that are threats to the United States and its interests but does not define assassination.

Evidence of the prohibition of assassinations appeared in military documents in 1863. General Order No. 100, also known as the Lieber Code, states: "The law of war does not allow proclaiming either an individual belonging to the hostile army, or a citizen, or a subject of the hostile government an outlaw, who may be slain without trial by any captor, any more than the modern law of peace allows such international outlawry; on the contrary, it abhors such outrage. The sternest retaliation should follow the murder committed in consequence of such proclamation, made by whatever authority. Civilized nations look with horror upon offers of rewards for the assassination of enemies as relapses into barbarism" (War Department 1863, 14). This order prohibited all assassinations, not just those conducted treacherously. Here, the Army declared all assassinations to be illegal even though international law stated only those done treacherously.

Current Army doctrine prohibiting assassination can be found in Field Manual 27-10, *Law of Land Warfare*, dated 1956. Paragraph 31 states "It is especially forbidden to kill or wound treacherously individuals belonging to the hostile nation or army. This article is construed as prohibiting assassination, proscription, or outlawry of an enemy, or

33

putting a price upon an enemy's head, as well as offering a reward for an enemy 'dead or alive'. It does not, however, preclude attacks on individual soldiers or officers of the enemy whether in the zone of hostilities, occupied territory, or elsewhere" (Department of the Army 1956, 17). This doctrine prohibits only those assassinations conducted treacherously thus coinciding with international law. However, it does not define treacherous nor assassination.

For centuries international law regarding assassinations has been debated. In the thirteenth century, Hugo Grotius and Emer de Vattel debated over the morality of assassination. These scholars found it acceptable to assassinate enemies as long as it was not done treacherously (Harder, 2002, 7). Emer de Vattel went on to say that assassination was contrary to law and honor (Zengel 1991, 128). In the seventeenth century, Alberico Gentili also debated over the question of assassination. He condemned killing sovereigns because of its absence of valor and the possibility that it could result in general disorder (Zengel 1991, 126). These early scholars agreed that killing an enemy was a legitimate form of warfare as long as it was not done treacherously. They were bound by the idea of honorable warfare and a desire to protect sovereigns.

Customary law also dates back centuries and is the oldest form of international law. Customary law is a body of unwritten law which is firmly established by the custom of nations (Department of the Army 1956, 4). These are rules that are recognized informally by a majority of nations and considered binding on these nations. The customary law regarding assassinations could also be referred to as an informal contract between gentlemen. Sovereigns declared themselves immune from attack thus exempt from assassination. This informal agreement precluded them from being targeted for assassination which would be deemed a violation of honor and justice (Zengel 1991, 126). Nor would they target another sovereign. This would protect kings and allow them to exercise their prerogatives as rulers (Zengel 1991, 127). In the dynastic armies of these times, war was fought by soldiers who were the property of the sovereigns.

The United Nations Charter also addresses assassination. Article 2(4) states: "All Members shall refrain in their international relations from the threat or use of force against the territorial integrity or political independence of any state, or in any other manner inconsistent with the Purposes of the United Nations" (1945, 1). This article prohibits the use of force against another nation, as well as against its leader.

Article 51 of the United Nations Charter addresses a nation's right to self-defense. It states "Nothing in the present Charter shall impair the inherent right of individual or collective self-defense if an armed attack occurs against a Member of the United Nations, until the Security Council has taken measures necessary to maintain international peace and security. Measures taken by Members in the exercise of this right of self-defense shall be immediately reported to the Security Council and shall not in any way affect the authority and responsibility of the Security Council under the present Charter to take at any time such action as it deems necessary in order to maintain or restore international peace and security" (United Nations 1945, 3). Article 51 allows the right of self-defense for the nation under attack as well as the nations coming to its assistance. For example, the United States exercised this right when coming to Kuwait's aid after the Iraqi invasion in August 1990.

"The US interpretation of Article 51 recognizes three general forms of self-defense: (1) self-defense against an actual use of force or hostile act; (2) preemptive self-defense against an imminent use of force; and (3) self-defense against a continuing threat" (Johnson 1992, 420). Through the use of sophisticated technology in the intelligence disciplines, knowledge of an impending attack has increased which allows the United States to respond prior to an imminent attack. Assassination can be legally justified as an act of preemptive self-defense against an imminent or continuing threat to the United States, its interests, and its citizens.

The United Nations also adopted the Convention on the Prevention and Punishment of Crimes Against Internationally Protected Persons, Including Diplomatic Agents on 14 December 1973 (Ku 1979, 853). This convention defines internationally protected persons as Heads of State, Heads of Government, or Ministers of Foreign Affairs (Ku 1979, 854). Article 2 of this convention also directs treaty nations to make assassination of internationally protected persons punishable under their own domestic law (Ku 1979, 855). This convention does not stipulate peacetime or wartime. Therefore, this treaty prohibits assassination of internationally protected persons at all times.

### The Moral Argument

There are clearly two opposing camps regarding assassination - those for and those against. The arguments center on the principles of legality, proportionality, necessity, the golden rule, and values. The legal arguments of assassination have already been addressed.

Proponents argue that assassination is lawful and moral as long as it meets the concepts of proportionality and necessity. The principle of proportionality means "the anticipated loss of life and damage to property incidental to attacks must not be excessive in relation to the concrete and direct military advantage expected to be gained" (ST 27-1

36

2001, 5-8). The objectives must be proportionate to the anticipated military advantage, meaning the benefits must outweigh the cost in lives and property. Proponents of assassination say killing one is proportionate while killing many is not. This principle advocates minimizing collateral damage including innocent civilians. They would also argue as to why other people should suffer because of one person. When the United States government applies the instruments of power, they affect more than just one person. For example, when applying the economic instrument of power, specifically economic sanctions, these affect the citizens of a country. Generally the targeted leader continues to enjoy a much higher standard of living while the standard for the average citizens drops significantly because of the disincentives being applied. Using the example of Saddam Hussein and Iraq, proportionality would mean targeting and eliminating him versus killing many Iraqi military and civilians while applying military force to remove him from power. The military principle of proportionality clearly favors assassination.

The concept of proportionality raises the question of the assassination of Archduke Francis-Ferdinand, known as the man whose assassination touched off World War I. Archduke Ferdinand, heir to the Austro-Hungarian throne, was shot by a member of a Serbian nationalist group (Addington 1994, 134). Even though his assassination did not stop the conflict between Austria and Serbia, it did not start World War I. It is the opinion of this author that World War I was caused by fervent nationalism. The entire continent was engulfed into war due to the alliances. Thus, using the assassination of Archduke Ferdinand as a rationale for not allowing assassination is without foundation.

Now, let us look at the concept of military necessity. Military necessity is the principle which justifies the measures which are "indispensable for securing the complete submission of the enemy as soon as possible" (Department of the Army 1956, 4). The target to be attacked must be absolutely necessary to accomplish the military's mission. Again looking at Saddam Hussein and Iraq, targeting him must achieve the United States objective of disarming Iraq and liberating the Iraqi people to meet the military principle of necessity. In order to achieve necessity, targeting Hussein would need to be an integral part of the United States mission. On the contrary, can the mission be achieved without eliminating a specific target, in this case an individual? If the answer is yes, then the target does not meet the rule of military necessity. Every operation is different, but in the case of Iraq, an argument could be made that Hussein and his regime are their center of gravity, thus attacking him should eliminate the Iraqi military's will to fight.

When the immediate threat of an individual is eliminated, who will succeed him? There is no way to predict who would succeed the targeted individual and what his position towards the United States would be. In 1989, former President Bush opposed Manuel Noriega and his regime of Panamanian Defense Forces. The United States wanted him ousted from power but considered all the Panamanian Defense Force leaders to be power hungry thugs (Woodward 1991, 133). Prior to Operation Just Cause, the plan included secretly swearing in Endara as President, the legitimate winner of the May election, to legitimize our military operation and bring about democracy (Woodward 1991, 170). When the United States military forces removed the Taliban from power in Afghanistan, it placed Hamid Karzai into power. Unfortunately, Karzai is seen as a United States puppet among the different tribes in Afghanistan. Normally, the United States is not in a position to choose a successor, especially one who will act favorably towards the United States. Killing individuals will merely eliminate the immediate threat.

38

The next argument is the concept of the Golden Rule: "Do unto others as you would have them do unto you". The concept of the Golden Rule raises the question of possible retribution. If the United States adopts the tactic of assassination, the international community could then be justified in targeting American leaders. For example, former President Bush's targeting of Saddam Hussein during Desert Storm resulted in an assassination attempt on President Bush in 1993 (Lowry 2002, 38). The United States cannot idly stand by and allow individuals to threaten our security and interests for fear of retaliation. The government must be proactive in protecting its security, interests, and citizens while ensuring that our leaders are protected from possible retribution. The President of the United States is probably the most heavily guarded individual in the world.

Crimes like assassination cannot only lead to possible retribution but to a cycle of violence. Israel and Palestine are perfect examples of violence leading to more violence. Opponents of assassination would argue that Israel's open assassination policy has failed to stop terrorism. The Israel-Palestinian conflict will be discussed later in detail.

The final argument questions whether assassination is compatible with the democratic ideals and values upon which this country was founded. In 1975, the Senate Committee determined that "the acts which it has examined do not represent the real American character. They do not reflect the ideals which have given the people of this country and of the world hope for a better, fuller, fairer life" (U.S. Congress, Senate 1975, 285). Americans feel the constitutional rights and freedoms they possess should be extended to all mankind, regardless of citizenship. The concepts of life, liberty, and the pursuit of happiness are incompatible with assassination.

Even though the individual threat may be a tyrant, opponents feel the United States should not resort to their tyrannical ways by killing more people. If the tyrant is guilty of crimes against humanity or other international crimes, he should be arrested not assassinated. Unfortunately, an international criminal court system to try such individuals does not exist (Beres 1995, 1). This raises the question of whether or not the United States has the right to arrest foreign nationals guilty of such crimes. Precedence has been set allowing the United States to arrest foreign criminals. The United States arrested, tried, convicted, and jailed Manuel Noriega on drug trafficking charges. The United States has also detained hundreds of suspected terrorists in Guantanamo Bay, Cuba for over a year.

## Israel--A Case Study

The Israeli-Palestinian conflict dates back to the declaration of the Israeli state in 1948. At the heart of the conflict are ancient claims to the land by both Israelis and Palestinians. Palestinians have resorted to suicide bombings in their quest for the land. The Israeli government retaliates by killing suspected terrorists. Then it starts all over again with more death and destruction. A recent example includes a Palestinian blowing up a bus in Israel. Israel retaliated by deploying its gunships to kill the leader of Hamas and his bodyguards (BBC News 2003, 1). Violence seems to beget more violence.

Do these killings qualify as assassination using the previously identified definition? The killings on both sides are intentional and premeditated. A Palestinian terrorist plans and targets innocent Israeli civilians in a public place. Israel counters with a planned and coordinated strike against Palestinian terrorists.

40

Both sides are conducting the murders for political purposes. Palestine thinks violence will force the Israeli government and people to return their holy land. Israel retaliates to defend the Israeli people and nation. Israel is definitely conducting these murders treacherously by disguising their agents as Arab men and women.

However, the murders do not qualify as assassination because the targeted individuals are not protected persons under the United Nations mandate. The Palestinians are killing average Israeli men, women, and children. Israel is killing suspected terrorists.

Even though the killings do not qualify as assassination, the conflict is still worthy of discussion. Israel's tactics could be called counterterrorism. Israel claims the right of self-defense in response to these suicide bombers. In the absence of an international criminal court system, the Israeli government is acting as judge, jury, and executioner.

The collateral damage is high on both sides. The Palestinians are killing Israeli citizens including women and children. Although Israel retaliates by targeting suspected terrorists, innocent people are usually killed in the crossfire. But Israel's open assassination policy has failed to stop these terrorists and suicide bombers.

### Threats

The United States has faced threats to its security and interests since its inception. These threats have ranged from one individual to an entire country. Threats can either be tangible or intangible, the latter meaning you cannot see or count them. Let us look at the threats the United States faces today.

Countries can clash over tangible issues like territorial rights, oil, and human rights. The threat could be one country or multiple countries. Several countries were identified as the axis of evil by President Bush during his State of the Union address in

41

January 2002. These countries were identified as threats because of their human rights violations, support of terrorists, and possession of weapons of mass destruction. These countries include Iraq, Iran, and North Korea.

Threats can also come in the form of a single individual. The United States has been faced with threats from individuals throughout history. Military leaders like Manuel Noriega have posed a threat to the United States. Noriega and his Panamanian Defense Forces were a threat to the Panama Canal, a vital interest to the United States. Non-state actors and rogue tribal leaders like Mohammed Farrah Aidid have threatened regional stability. Today the United States faces threats like Saddam Hussein, head of the Iraqi state and military, and Osama bin Laden, head of Al Qaeda.

Religion and ideology can be intangible threats. Many wars have been fought over religion, for example the Crusades and Arab-Israeli War just to name a few. Although religions do not typically preach violence, people distort theology by rationalizing the conduct of heinous acts in the name of their God. Today the United States is faced with the threat from Islamic radicals. Israel, a United States interest, faces the Arab and Palestinian threat.

Besides religion, ideology can cause clashes between societies. The Cold War is an excellent example where democracy clashed against communism. The clash between democracy and Islamic fundamentalism exists today.

### Eliminating Threats

The United States applies the diplomatic, information, military, and economic instruments of power to deal with threats to its national security and interests. The United States executes its foreign policy either directly or indirectly through these instruments of

42

power. Why would the United States resort to measures like assassination in dealing with its threats? The United States could resort to assassination in dealing with threats when it feels all other measures have failed. But can assassination eliminate the previously identified threats to the United States, its citizens, and interests?

Several tangible and intangible threats were identified above. The President identified countries like Iraq, Iran, and North Korea as threats to the United States. Assassination applies to individuals not groups of people or entire countries. Therefore, assassination would not eliminate these countries as threats. But should the United States target their leaders?

While assassination cannot eliminate an entire country as a threat, the next question is whether or not targeting its leader will. If Saddam Hussein and Kim Jong Il were assassinated, would their respective countries be eliminated as threats? One can argue that if a leader is his country's center of gravity, then eliminating him should therefore eliminate the country as a threat.

Military and foreign leaders are not the only threats to the United States. The United States faces asymmetric threats from non-state actors and rogue tribal leaders like Osama bin Laden. President Bush even went so far as publicly saying Osama bin Laden was wanted, "dead or alive," referring to the old western poster (Bush 2001, 3). Assassination would eliminate them as threats. But killing does not imply assassination. These individuals do not have status as protected persons under international law. Therefore, killing them would not qualify as assassination.

While killing specific individuals would eliminate them as threats, there is no way to predict who would succeed the targeted individual and what his position towards the

United States would be. For example, killing Saddam Hussein and Kim Jong Il does not mean the United States will be safe from their weapons of mass destruction. Nor will killing Osama bin Laden keep the United States safe from other extremist individuals or groups. Eliminating these leaders could possibly cause more domestic as well as international upheaval.

Can assassination eliminate intangible threats like religion and ideology? The answer is no. Assassination does not apply to entire groups of people, only to individuals. You cannot eliminate an entire religion or ideology by killing individuals although many have tried. This country stands for freedom of religion, speech, and beliefs. One can assume these freedoms extend to all mankind, not just Americans.

## Conclusion

This chapter presented the analysis of the topic of assassination. The legal and moral arguments were identified. Assassination was defined and current United States policy and international law examined. The views of the opposing camps regarding assassination were then presented. Israel and its open assassination policy were also discussed. Finally, assassination was applied to the threats facing the United States to determine whether or not they could be eliminated. The next chapter will present the conclusions drawn from this analysis.

# CHAPTER 5

## CONCLUSION

### Introduction

The previous chapter presented the analysis of the topic of assassination. There are many conclusions that can be drawn from this analysis. Legal and moral conclusions regarding assassination will be presented. Then recommendations for future research will be given. Finally, this chapter will address the primary question, "Can the United States assassinate an individual who poses a threat to its national security and interests?"

### Legal Conclusions

It is quite evident that assassination is illegal in accordance with domestic policy and international law. Executive Order 12333 bans assassination by any employee of the United States government. The Law of War, United Nations Charter, and Hague Convention also prohibit assassination.

The legal debate over assassination stems from the failure of Executive Order 12333 and international law to define assassination. The common themes among the different definitions include terms like public figure and political purpose. For lack of an agreed-upon definition, this thesis defined assassination as an intentional and premeditated killing of a protected person conducted treacherously for a political purpose.

The word assassination is misused by the media and general public. Defining assassination would clearly identify what is and, more importantly, what is not assassination. Using the previously identified definition of assassination, let us put the definition to the test with so-called assassinations from past history and potential future

45

targets. The murder of Martin Luther King, Jr. does not qualify as assassination because he was not a protected person under the United Nations mandate. To reiterate, a protected person is a Head of State, Head of Government, or Minister of Foreign Affairs (Ku 1979, 854).

If the CIA's plot to kill Fidel Castro of Cuba had been successful, it would have qualified as an assassination for several reasons. First and foremost, as head of his country, Castro qualified as a protected person. The several attempted plots were contrived to be treacherous using underworld figures. As a political objective, the United States government hoped Castro's elimination would contain communism and bring about democracy less than 100 miles from its borders. Therefore, the plot qualifies as assassination under the definition.

Does assassination apply to terrorists, rogue tribal leaders or drug traffickers? While the killing could be done treacherously and for a political purpose, these individuals do not have status as protected persons under international law. Therefore, targeting and killing these non-state actors would not qualify as assassination. Several threats fall under this category. As leader of an international terrorist network, Osama bin Laden is not a protected person. Neither would Abdullah Omar, the tribal leader in the opening hypothetical scenario, be considered a protected person.

Do the killings in the Israeli-Palestinian conflict qualify as assassination? The answer is no. While the killings are conducted for the political purpose of reclaiming ancient lands, these targets do not have status as protected persons under the United Nations mandate.

Having established who the United States can legally target, when is the United States legally justified to attack? The United States has interpreted Article 51 of the United Nations Charter to include the right of preemptive self-defense against an imminent or continuing threat. Intelligence to support such preemptive action has increased through advanced technology. With positive proof of such an impending attack, the United States would be legally justified in any necessary action taken to defend its country and citizens. The actions taken must meet the military principles of proportionality and necessity. Now the legal conclusions approach the moral and philosophical debate.

## Moral Conclusions

The moral conclusions can be divided into the principles of legality, proportionality, necessity, the golden rule, and values. First, assassination definitely meets the concept of proportionality. The benefits of military objectives like conducting assassination must outweigh the cost in lives and property. Killing one is clearly proportionate while killing many is not. As opposed to applying conventional military force, assassination can preserve the lives of soldiers, both friendly and enemy, and non-combatants. Targeting and killing one specific individual minimizes collateral damage in terms of civilians and property. Applying other instruments of power like economic, does not meet this concept because it makes many suffer for the actions of one or a few. Assassination is a way to deal with bad people to prevent greater evil.

The concept of proportionality with regard to assassination implies that killing one will prevent the loss of further lives. Assassination should be used to stop further conflict and the loss of lives, not precipitate it. Let us look at the assassination of

47

Archduke Francis-Ferdinand in 1914. Archduke Ferdinand is incorrectly noted as the man whose assassination resulted in World War I. Again, it is the author's opinion that Archduke Ferdinand's assassination did not cause World War I and the loss of thousands of lives. War had been inevitable due to nationalism and the existing alliances.

Military necessity requires each objective to be crucial to accomplishing the overall mission. Assassination would be a strategic decision not a tactical one. The individual should only be targeted if his elimination would accomplish the national strategic objectives. This would certainly be the case if the targeted individual was identified as the enemy's center of gravity. This means the individual is a source of power from which a military force derives its freedom of action, physical strength, or will to fight ( Joint Chiefs of Staff 2001). Taking it one step further, without this individual, the military force would become vulnerable and weaker. The enemy's will to fight, source of power, and freedom of action would all be destroyed. Assassination would meet the military principle of necessity if the targeted individual was identified as the enemy's center of gravity and eliminating him were crucial to accomplishing national strategic objectives.

Another moral argument is that we should treat others as we would like others to treat us. Some argue that assassination could result in retaliation and lead to a cycle of violence. Fear of retaliation should never dictate foreign policy. The United States should not idly stand by and wait for possible attacks on its interests and citizens for fear of what could happen. The 11th of September showed the United States that surprise can still be achieved against this modern and technologically advanced state. The United States government, specifically the Secret Service, should continue to safeguard its leaders. The

President of the United States is the most heavily guarded man in the world with access to the most advanced technology to identify and deter an attack and, if necessary, respond in kind. While some allege the attacks in the Israeli-Palestinian conflict lead to a cycle of violence, the author disagrees. Regardless of the actions taken by the Israeli government, the Palestinians will continue to conduct terrorist attacks believing it will achieve their objective of a Palestinian state on holy land.

Lastly, the author will agree that assassination is incompatible with the democratic ideals and values upon which this country was founded. But the previous arguments, especially the principle of proportionality, far outweigh the compromise of values. Being faced with a threat, it would be more acceptable morally to kill one individual than many soldiers and civilians when applying military force. Assassination is a more precise weapon than deploying large conventional forces.

## Recommendations

The historical background leading up to the executive order banning assassination was wrought with questionable activities by the United States government. There were alleged killings of innocent women and children during the Vietnam War. And the CIA was involved in assassination plots involving foreign leaders. This was a very moral self-righteous time in the United States. President Ford acquiesced to the pressure from Congress and the American people by publicly stating in an executive order that his government would not conduct assassinations.

Executive Order 12333 is a policy directed by the President not a law imposed by Congress. The executive order is a policy statement made by the President openly stating his government will not conduct assassinations. There are several courses of action

49

regarding this policy. First, leave it alone and continue the policy ban on assassinations. Second, send it to Congress to be enacted as a law. Third, revise it, define assassination, and delineate conditions that must be met to target specific individuals with the required approval of the President. Fourth, rescind it to allow the government to either openly or covertly assassinate threats to the United States and its interests. The author recommends the fourth option.

The executive order has definitely outlived its utility. It may have been appropriate twenty-five years ago but not in the global war on terrorism today. The executive order is antiquated and based on the conventional threats of the past not the asymmetric threats of today. The executive order leads to confusion over what constitutes assassination because its failure to define assassination. The public ban on assassination also limits the President's flexibility in dealing with rogue threats. Rescinding it would not only clarify United States policy on assassination, it could also act as a deterrent to potential threats to the United States.

Why would the United States resort to such a measure as assassination? Obviously the diplomatic, information, and economic instruments of power would be exhausted prior to such an act. The instruments of power are relevant against non-state actors, either directly or indirectly. The United States stance is not to negotiate with terrorists nor lend legitimacy to a terrorist organization. The United States could apply diplomatic pressure against countries so they do not harbor the terrorists or narco-terrorists. The information instrument could be used in the form of campaigns for citizens to stop supporting the terrorists. Economically, the United States could cut off their funding sources to limit their resources to attack our nation or interests. Or use economic

50

sanctions to apply pressure on citizens to remove support from the terrorists. But all these instruments of power affect many while assassination just affects one. Assassination could be an effective tool in dealing with threats from rogue leaders. Killing non-state actors to protect national security is also advocated, although it would not qualify as assassination.

According to the National Security Strategy, the United States reserves the right to preempt countries that possess weapons of mass destruction with the potential of threatening their neighbors or the United States. The United States also reserves the right to preempt rogue states that harbor terrorists. Assassination could be the perfect tool of preemption.

Because assassination is a strategic weapon, its potential use would be bestowed upon the National Security Council. They would debate its use to target specific individuals requiring the ultimate approval of the President.

### Recommendations for Future Research

Research could lead to several other topics. Several ideas are absent from the recommendations above. Although this thesis does not engage in these topics, research may be warranted in these areas. Who will be the executive agent to conduct assassination? Some possible agents include the CIA, the military, or maybe even hired mercenaries. If caught while executing the mission, what fate would befall these agents? The United States government may be conducting assassination overtly or covertly, in which case they could possibly disavow any knowledge of the operation, leaving the agents out on their own.

Another idea for further research could be the possibility of targeting a United States citizen for assassination. If the threat were a United States citizen, would the United States government still order his assassination? And if so, would this assassination be conducted on United States soil? While Executive Order 12333 bans assassination, it was also enacted to protect the constitutional rights of United States persons. The United States government is restricted in its collection on United States persons. Americans enjoy many privileges without the fear of electronic surveillance and unconsented physical searches. These laws do not currently extend to foreigners on United States or foreign soil.

## Conclusion

This final chapter has presented the legal and moral conclusions when analyzing assassination. It also provided recommendations to codify the United States policy on assassination and ideas for future research. This thesis has researched whether the United States can assassinate an individual who poses a threat to its national security and interests. Today's war on terrorism calls for drastic measures to fight asymmetric threats. The author concludes that the United States should reserve the option of assassination of its threats as a tool of foreign policy.

# REFERENCE LIST

Addington, Larry H. 1994. *The Patterns of War Since the Eighteenth Century.* Bloomington, IN: Indiana University Press.

BBC News. 2003. "Killing of Hamas leader 'justified'," 9 March. Available from newsvote.bbc.co.uk/mpapps/pagetools/print/news.bbc.co.uk/1/hi/world/middle_ea st. Internet. Accessed on 20 May 2003.

Beres, Louis Rene. 1995. "Assassination of Terrorists may be Law-enforcing," 31 October. Available from www.professors.org.il/docs/beres3.htm. Internet. Accessed on 1 October 2002.

Beres, Louis Rene. 2003. Assassinations: Getting them First. *Chicago Tribune,* 2 February.

Bolchoz, J. Manning, Lieutenant Colonel. 1999. *Center of Gravity: Justification for Assassination?* Carlisle Barracks, PA: US Army War College.

Buchanan, Patrick J. 2002. Do we have a License to Kill? *Creators Syndicate, Inc.*, 19 June.

Bush, George W. 2002. "President Delivers State of the Union Address" (speech delivered at the United States Capitol on 29 January). Available from www.whitehouse.gov/news/release/2002/01/print/20020129-11.htm. Internet. Accessed on 10 January 2003.

Cassel, Doug. 2003. Repercussions: An Eye for an Eye. *Chicago Tribune,* 2 February.

Department of the Army. 1956. Field Manual 27-10, *The Law of Land Warfare.* Washington, DC: US Government Printing Office.

Filiss, John. n.d. "War by Assassination." Available from http://www.primitivism.com/ assassination.htm. Internet. Accessed on 10 October 2002.

Friedman, Leon, ed. 1972. *The Law of War: A Documentary History – Volume I.* New York: Random House.

Harder, Tyler J., Major. 2002. Time to Repeal the Assassination Ban of Executive Order 12,333: A Small Step in Clarifying Current Law. *Military Law Review* 172 (June): 1-39.

Herbert, Roger G., Jr. 1992. *Bullets With Names: The Deadly Dilemma.* Monterey, CA: Naval Postgraduate School.

Hoffman, Michael A. II. n.d. "Jewish Assassination and Media Doublethink." Available from http://www.hoffman-info.com/palestine49.html. Internet. Accessed on 10 October 2002.

Irvin, Victor D., Lieutenant Colonel. 2002, *Political Assassination, The Strategic Precision Weapon of Choice*. Carlisle Barracks, PA: US Army War College.

Johnson, Boyd M. III. 1992. Executive Order 12,333: the Permissibility of an American Assassination of a Foreign Leader. *Cornell International Law Journal* 25 (spring): 401-35.

Joint Chiefs of Staff. 2001. Joint Publication 3-0, *Doctrine for Joint Operations*. Washington, DC: US Government Printing Office.

Kafala, Tarik. 2001. "Israel's 'assassination policy',"1 August. Available from news. bbc.co.uk/1/hi/world/middle_east/1258187.stm. Internet. Accessed on 1 October 2002.

Keller, Alvin W., Jr., Lieutenant Colonel. 1992. *Targeting the Head of State during the Gulf War Conflict: A Legal Analysis*. Newport, RI: Naval War College.

Kelley, Jack. 2001. 'We're going to get them': Israel hunts terrorists amid controversy. *USA Today*, 21 August.

Ku, Min-Chuan, Dr., ed. 1979. *A Comprehensive Handbook of the United Nations: A Documentary Presentation in Two Volumes*. New York: Monarch Press.

Lowry, Richard. 2002. A View to a Kill. *National Review* 54: 36-38.

Metz, Steven. 2001. "Strategic Asymmetry." Available from http://www.cgsc.army.mil/milrev/English/JulAug01/met.asp. Internet. Accessed on 9 August 2002.

Pape, Matthew S. 2002. Can We Put the Leaders of the "Axis of Evil" in the Crosshairs? *Parameters* (autumn): 62-71.

Student Text 27-1. 2001. *Military Law*. Fort Leavenworth, KS: US Army Command and General College.

Thomas, Evan, and John Barry. 2001. Evil in the Crosshairs. *Newsweek Magazine*, 24 December, 10-20.

U.S. Congress, Senate. 1975. *Alleged Assassination Plots Involving Foreign Leaders*. 94th Cong., 1st sess.

U.S. President. 1976. Executive Order. United States Foreign Intelligence Activities, Executive Order 11905. *Federal Register* 12, no. 8 (23 February).

U.S. President. 1981. Executive Order. United States Intelligence Activities, Executive Order 12333. Available from http://www.fas.org/irp/offdocs/eo12333.htm. Internet. Accessed on 3 September 2002.

United Nations. 1945. "Charter of the United Nations," 26 June. Available from http://www.un.org/Overview/Charter.html. Internet. Accessed on 20 May 2002.

War Department. 1863. "The Lieber Code of 1863" 24 April. Available from http://www.civilWarhome.com/liebercode.htm. Internet. Accessed on 20 May 2003.

*Webster's Ninth New Collegiate Dictionary*. 1984. Springfield, MA: Merriam-Webster Inc.

Weinberger, Caspar W. 2001. When Can We Target the Leaders? *Strategic Review* (spring): 21-4.

Woodward, Bob. 1991. *The Commanders*. New York: Simon and Schuster.

Zengel, Patricia, Lieutenant Commander. 1991. Assassination and the Law of Armed Conflict. *Military Law Review* 134 (fall): 123-55.